It was games time at school. The children were outside on the field. Anneena ran up to Mrs May.

"Come and see something, Mrs May," she said.

Someone had broken the fence down and dumped junk on the field. Wilf was cross.

"We don't want junk on our field," he said.

"The field isn't a dump," said Mrs May.

Then Mrs May saw something in the junk.

"Do you see this?" she asked the children. "It's a mangle. It gets the water out of wet clothes."

"How does it do that?" asked Anneena.

Mrs May took the mangle into the classroom. She showed the children how it worked. First she got a big sheet and made it wet. Then Nadim turned the handle and Biff helped Mrs May put the sheet through.

The water ran out of the sheet and went into a bucket.

"We don't use mangles now to get clothes dry," said Mrs May. "What do we use?"

Mrs May showed the children a picture of someone washing clothes a long time ago. Mrs May asked the children if they had any old things at home. Some of the children said they had.

When Biff and Chip got home from school they looked at the little house.

"The house looks very old," said Chip, "and so do these little children. Let's take them to school."

Kipper didn't want them to take the little house to school.

"What about the magic?" he asked Biff.

"The magic won't work if we don't take the key," said Biff.

Some of the children took old things to school.

"What a lot of things," said Mrs May. "We can find out all about them and have a display."

Mrs May liked the little house and so did all the children. Biff and Chip didn't say that the house was magic. That was a secret.

Wilf was being silly. He climbed on Mrs May's table and pushed some books over. The books fell on to the little house with a crash.

"Oh no!" said Biff.

One of the books made a hole in the roof. Wilf was very upset when he saw that the roof was broken.

"I'm sorry," he said. "Perhaps I can get my dad to mend it."

Biff and Chip took the house home. Kipper was cross when he saw that it was broken. He had the magic key in his hand.

"Will the magic still work?" he asked. Just then the key began to glow.

A new adventure began. The magic took the children back in time. It took them to their house a long time ago. The house looked new but the roof was broken.

There were three children playing outside and two men were mending the roof.

"Didn't our house look nice a long time ago?" said Biff. "But how did the roof get broken?"

The children saw Biff, Chip and Kipper, and ran up to them.

"Hello," they said. "Who are you?"

"I'm Biff," said Biff. "This is Chip, and this is Kipper."

“What funny names!” said the girl. “My name is Victoria, this is Edward, and this is Will.”

“What funny clothes you have!” said Will.

“Not as funny as yours!” said Kipper.

Kipper looked up at the men on the roof.

"How did the roof get broken?" he asked.

"We don't know," said Edward. "It was broken when we woke up."

"That's funny," said Kipper.

A lady came out and called to the children.

"Go inside and wash your hands," she said. "It's time for tea."

"Is that your mother?" Biff asked.

"No," said Edward. "That's our cook."

The children went into the kitchen. The cook looked at Biff, Chip and Kipper.

"May they stay to tea?" asked Victoria.

"They have funny clothes," said Cook, "but yes."

Biff looked round the kitchen.

"This is not like our kitchen," she said.

Cook looked at Chip's hands.

"Go and wash your hands," she said.

"You can't have tea until you do."

After tea, Cook made the children wash their hands again. Then she told Edward to take some tea to the workmen.

"Come and see our rooms," said Edward.

The broken roof was in Edward's room.
"Is it mended yet?" he asked.
"It won't be long now," said the man.
"Thanks for the tea."

The children went into Victoria's room. Victoria had a little room in her bedroom. It was the one Biff had.

"We keep toys in here," said Victoria. "Come and look."

Biff, Chip, and Kipper looked at the children's toys.

"I wish we had a horse like this," he said.

"So do I," said Biff.

Victoria took Biff, Chip, and Kipper into the little room.

"Come and see this," she said.

"What is it?" asked Kipper.

Victoria showed them a little house. She told them that her father was making it for them.

"It will look like this house," she said.

"We know," said Biff.

Edward looked at Chip's watch and Chip looked at Edward's boat.

"Do you want to swap?" asked Edward.

"Yes, please," said Chip, "then I can take the boat to school to show Mrs May."

Suddenly the magic key began to glow.

"It's time to go," said Kipper, "but I don't want to."

"Will you come back?" asked Edward.

"We don't know," said Biff. "Maybe."

The magic took the children home. They looked at the little house.

"The broken roof has been mended," said Biff. "How did that happen?"

“I don’t know,” said Chip, “maybe Dad mended it.”

“I think the workmen in the adventure did it,” said Kipper. “We saw them.”

“I think it was magic,” said Biff.

“I liked that adventure best of all,” said Biff. “I liked those children long ago. I’d like to go back and see them again.”

“Me too,” said Chip, looking at the boat. “Maybe I could get my watch back!”